Practice to Learn

ADDITION AND SUBTRACTION

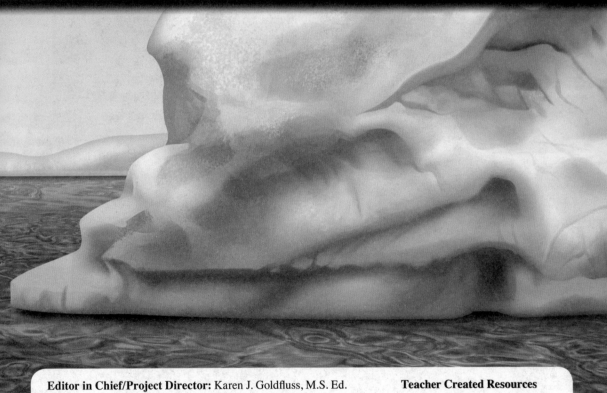

Editor in Chief/Project Director: Karen J. Goldfluss, M.S. Ed.

Editor: Eric Migliaccio

Author: Eric Migliaccio

Imaging: James Edward Grace

Cover and Interior Design: Sarah Kim

Art Coordinator: Renee Mc Elwee

Creative Director: Sarah M. Fournier

Publisher: Mary D. Smith, M.S. Ed.

Teacher Created Resources
12621 Western Avenue
Garden Grove, CA 92841
Printed in U.S.A.

www.teachercreated.com
ISBN: 978-1-4206-8224-3
©2019 Teacher Created Resources
Made in U.S.A.

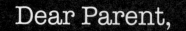

Dear Parent,

This book is part of the *Practice to Learn* series for young learners. Each vibrant book in the series includes a wide range of interesting activities that will help your child develop essential foundational skills. Written by experienced teachers and educators, the series supports what your child learns at school.

The pages are clear and uncluttered, with activities that build real skills. Activities are fun and motivate children to continue working and learning. Instructions are clear and easy to follow.

We hope that you and your child enjoy using this and other books in the series.

Contents

At-Home Activities	4
Addition Table	6
Subtraction Tables	7
Addition Activities	8–13, 18, 26, 28–29, 32, 34, 36, 39, 42, 45, 50–51, 60–61
Subtraction Activities	19–22, 24, 27, 30–31, 33, 35, 37, 43
Addition and Subtraction Activities	14–17, 23, 25, 38, 40–41, 44, 46–49, 52–59
Number Line Activities	28–31
Word Problems	22, 38, 44–45, 53, 56–57
Puzzles and Games	41, 58–61
Answer Key	62
Cool! Award Certificate	64

Addition and Subtraction Activities

Use what you already have and what you already do in and around the house to help your child practice and learn addition and subtraction at home. Use these ideas to get children thinking about math in a way that makes sense to them.

Idea #1: Start with addition before moving on to subtraction. Addition is an easier concept to grasp.

Idea #2: Use three main methods to help your child understand addition. Use fingers, small objects, and pictures.

▶ **Fingers** — When it comes to learning addition, fingers can sure be handy! For very young learners, keep the finger counting to one hand by giving simple addition problems that add up to no more than 5. Once your child is able to make the connection that the fingers on the second hand are a continuation of the fingers on the first, give math problems with sums between 6 and 10.

▶ **Small Objects** — Once your child begins to get the hang of finger adding (and subtracting), start to use small objects. Demonstrate how you can count a certain number of objects (for example, 4) and then add more objects (for example, 3) to that group. By counting the total number of objects now in the group, you are doing addition (for example, 4 + 3 = 7).

▶ **Drawing Pictures** — Another way to demonstrate addition is by having your child draw a certain number of objects (for example, 2 fish) and then draw more objects alongside the original group (for example, 3 fish). Your child can then count the total number of objects to find out what the two numbers added together equal (for example, 2 + 3 = 5).

Idea #3: Once your child has shown some mastery of simple addition, introduce subtraction and its inverse relationship with addition. Addition tells you how many things there are all together. Subtraction helps you know how many things remain once you take some away. Try this tasty way to demonstrate subtraction:

▶ **Snack Subtraction** — Let your child choose a small snack, such as fish crackers, cereal pieces, or raisins. Count out 10 of the snack food. After allowing your child to eat some of the snacks, ask how many are left. Write a number sentence to reflect the snack subtraction.

...ition and Subtraction Games

Double Hop — Draw a hopscotch grid. Put numbers 1–10 in the squares. While hopping on a square, your child must hop twice on each number and say the doubles math fact. For example, your child would hop twice on the 1 and say, "One plus one is two," before moving on to the next square. The math fact must be said correctly for the game to continue.

Fishin' for Addition — To begin, get a deck of regular playing cards and remove the 10s and face cards. (Leave the aces and explain to your child that these are each worth 1.) As in Go Fish, the object is to collect as many pairs as you can. But in this version, pairs are created when the numbers add up to 10.

Each player starts with five cards. On a turn, a player must ask for a number that, when added to one of the cards in their hand, adds up to 10. If the player gets it, the pair is kept and the player goes again. If not, the player can take a card from the pile. Play continues until all the cards are paired.

Subtraction Slight of Hand — Count out 10 small objects (like dried beans, buttons, or coins). While your child is not looking, cover some of the objects with a cup. Your child then has to use subtraction to figure out how many you've hidden.

Beachball Math — Write the numbers 1–10 all over an inflated beachball. Mix up where you put the numbers on the ball so that consecutive numbers aren't next to one another. Then, standing across from your child, toss the ball back and forth. The person who catches the ball must add (or subtract) the numbers closest to their thumbs. Say the numbers, then say the sum (or difference).

Add It Up, Knock It Down — Turn your wooden-block tower game into addition and subtraction practice. Using small sticker labels, write out addition and subtraction facts on the ends of the wooden blocks. These facts should use single-digit numbers.

Some examples: $8 + 7$, $6 + 9$, $4 + 3$, $7 - 2$, $3 - 1$, $9 - 5$

Let your child go first. For this version of the game, rather than finding a block that feels loose, your child will need to find a math fact and answer it quickly! Before removing the block from the tower, your child needs to provide the correct answer.

Addition Table

+	1	2	3	4	5	6	7	8	9	10
1	2	3	4	5	6	7	8	9	10	11
2	3	4	5	6	7	8	9	10	11	12
3	4	5	6	7	8	9	10	11	12	13
4	5	6	7	8	9	10	11	12	13	14
5	6	7	8	9	10	11	12	13	14	15
6	7	8	9	10	11	12	13	14	15	16
7	8	9	10	11	12	13	14	15	16	17
8	9	10	11	12	13	14	15	16	17	18
9	10	11	12	13	14	15	16	17	18	19
10	11	12	13	14	15	16	17	18	19	20

Subtraction Tables

ONES
1 – 1 = 0
2 – 1 = 1
3 – 1 = 2
4 – 1 = 3
5 – 1 = 4
6 – 1 = 5
7 – 1 = 6
8 – 1 = 7
9 – 1 = 8

TWOS
2 – 2 = 0
3 – 2 = 1
4 – 2 = 2
5 – 2 = 3
6 – 2 = 4
7 – 2 = 5
8 – 2 = 6
9 – 2 = 7
10 – 2 = 8

THREES
3 – 3 = 0
4 – 3 = 1
5 – 3 = 2
6 – 3 = 3
7 – 3 = 4
8 – 3 = 5
9 – 3 = 6
10 – 3 = 7
11 – 3 = 8

FOURS
4 – 4 = 0
5 – 4 = 1
6 – 4 = 2
7 – 4 = 3
8 – 4 = 4
9 – 4 = 5
10 – 4 = 6
11 – 4 = 7
12 – 4 = 8

FIVES
5 – 5 = 0
6 – 5 = 1
7 – 5 = 2
8 – 5 = 3
9 – 5 = 4
10 – 5 = 5
11 – 5 = 6
12 – 5 = 7
13 – 5 = 8

SIXES
6 – 6 = 0
7 – 6 = 1
8 – 6 = 2
9 – 6 = 3
10 – 6 = 4
11 – 6 = 5
12 – 6 = 6
13 – 6 = 7
14 – 6 = 8

SEVENS
7 – 7 = 0
8 – 7 = 1
9 – 7 = 2
10 – 7 = 3
11 – 7 = 4
12 – 7 = 5
13 – 7 = 6
14 – 7 = 7
15 – 7 = 8

EIGHTS
8 – 8 = 0
9 – 8 = 1
10 – 8 = 2
11 – 8 = 3
12 – 8 = 4
13 – 8 = 5
14 – 8 = 6
15 – 8 = 7
16 – 8 = 8

NINES
9 – 9 = 0
10 – 9 = 1
11 – 9 = 2
12 – 9 = 3
13 – 9 = 4
14 – 9 = 5
15 – 9 = 6
16 – 9 = 7
17 – 9 = 8

TENS
10 – 10 = 0
11 – 10 = 1
12 – 10 = 2
13 – 10 = 3
14 – 10 = 4
15 – 10 = 5
16 – 10 = 6
17 – 10 = 7
18 – 10 = 8

Button Up

Count the buttons in each group. Add the groups together.

1.

Group 1	Group 2
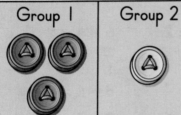	

_____ + _____ = _____

2.

Group 1	Group 2

_____ + _____ = _____

3.

Group 1	Group 2

_____ + _____ = _____

4.

Group 1	Group 2

_____ + _____ = _____

5.

Group 1	Group 2
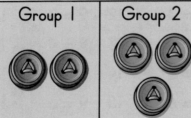	

_____ + _____ = _____

6.

Group 1	Group 2

_____ + _____ = _____

Adding Hearts

For each set of pictures, write an addition problem to match.

1.

_____ + _____ = _____

2.

_____ + _____ = _____

3.

_____ + _____ = _____

4.

_____ + _____ = _____

5.

_____ + _____ = _____

6.
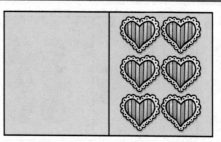

_____ + _____ = _____

Adding Apples

For each set of pictures, write an addition problem to match.

1.

_____ + _____ = _____

2.

_____ + _____ = _____

3.

_____ + _____ = _____

4.

_____ + _____ = _____

5.

_____ + _____ = _____

6.

_____ + _____ = _____

Let It Snow

Count each set of snowflakes. Add them up. Find the totals.

1. + = _____

2. + = _____

3.  + = _____

4.  + = _____

5.  +  = _____

Draw your own problem with snowflakes. Draw the numbers shown. Add up the snowflakes you draw. How many are there total?

Draw 2 snowflakes.		Draw 5 snowflakes.		
	+		=	

Time for Bed

Solve the addition problems. Match each pet to its correct bed.

8 + 3 = _____

10

0 + 10 = _____

12

7 + 5 = _____

13

9 + 4 = _____

11

A Sum of 20

Find two numbers that add up to 20. Find the first number on the left. Draw a line from that number to a number on the right that helps it add up to exactly 20. The first one is done for you.

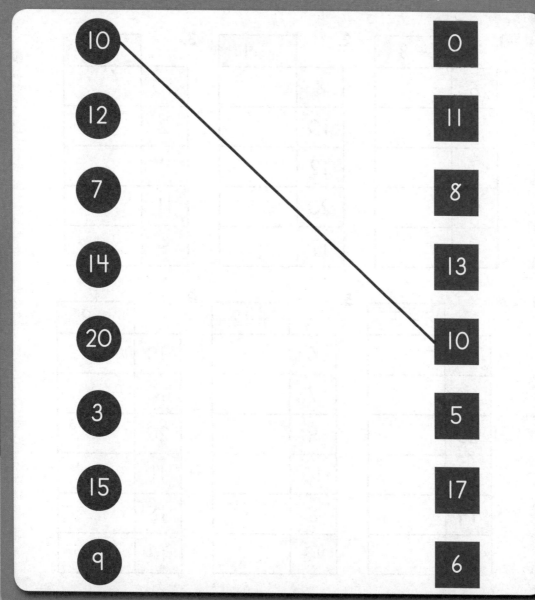

Math Machines

Each box below is a math machine. Each has a number and sign (+ or −) at the top. Add that number to or subtract it from the rest of the numbers in the machine.

1.

	+ 3
6	
5	
7	
9	
11	

2.

	− 4
8	
10	
12	
20	
17	

3.

	+ 9
10	
2	
9	
11	
6	

4.

	− 5
8	
10	
20	
16	
14	
11	

5.

	+ 12
6	
7	
9	
10	
8	
12	

6.

	− 9
19	
10	
20	
11	
18	
13	

Odd or Even?

Solve the problems below.
- If the answer is even, color the space green.
- If the answer is odd, color the space red.

1.
$$10 + 1$$

2.
$$9 - 1$$

3.
$$13 + 3$$

4.
$$11 - 1$$

5.
$$12 - 11$$

6.
$$15 + 4$$

7.
$$11 + 9$$

8.
$$7 - 6$$

9.
$$19 - 14$$

10.
$$20 + 2$$

11.
$$23 + 0$$

12.
$$16 - 9$$

More or Less?

Solve each side of each problem. Use the correct symbol to show which side has more (or if the sides are equal).

Remember:

> means **"greater than"**   < means **"less than"**   = means **"equal to"**

Addition Problems

1. $3 + 6$ ◯ $5 + 5$

2. $7 + 2$ ◯ $3 + 4$

3. $11 + 1$ ◯ $10 + 3$

4. $6 + 7$ ◯ $0 + 13$

5. $10 + 5$ ◯ $6 + 6$

6. $8 + 11$ ◯ $5 + 15$

Subtraction Problems

7. $6 - 6$ ◯ $5 - 5$

8. $7 - 2$ ◯ $10 - 4$

9. $11 - 1$ ◯ $10 - 3$

10. $10 - 7$ ◯ $8 - 6$

11. $16 - 5$ ◯ $18 - 9$

12. $13 - 1$ ◯ $15 - 3$

Write Your Own: Create your own problem. Write an addition or subtraction problem on each side. Then write in the correct symbol to show which side is greater.

_____   _____ ◯ _____   _____

Mixed-Up More or Less?

Solve each side of each problem. Use the correct symbol to show which side has more (or if the sides are equal).

Remember:

> means **"greater than"**   < means **"less than"**   = means **"equal to"**

1. $3 + 6$ ◯ $15 - 5$

2. $7 - 2$ ◯ $3 + 4$

3. $13 + 1$ ◯ $14 - 2$

4. $7 + 6$ ◯ $13 - 0$

5. $10 + 5$ ◯ $20 - 6$

6. $1 + 11$ ◯ $15 - 4$

7. $1 + 0$ ◯ $15 - 3$

8. $17 - 2$ ◯ $11 + 4$

9. $11 - 1$ ◯ $9 + 2$

10. $10 + 7$ ◯ $18 - 2$

11. $16 + 1$ ◯ $18 - 0$

12. $13 + 1$ ◯ $15 - 1$

Write Your Own: Create your own problem. Write an addition problem on one side and a subtraction problem on the other. Then write in the correct symbol to show which side is greater.

_____ _____ ◯ _____ _____

Adding Dots

Finish the addition sentences. Write the answers. Draw the dots.

1.

4 dots plus 2 dots = _____ dots

• • + • =
• •   •

2.

3 dots plus 5 dots = _____ dots

• • + • • • =
 •   • •

3.

8 dots plus 1 dot = _____ dots

• • • • + • =
• • • •

4.

6 dots plus 6 dots = _____ dots

• • • + • • • =
• • •   • • •

5.

6 dots plus 9 dots = _____ dots

• • • + • • • • • =
• • •   • • • •

6.

10 dots plus 10 dots = _____ dots

• • • • • + • • • • • =
• • • • •   • • • • •

Subtracting Dots

Finish the subtraction sentences. Write the answers. Draw the dots.

1.

4 dots take away 2 dots = _____ dots

:: – : =

2.

5 dots take away 4 dots = _____ dot

•:: – :: =

3.

8 dots take away 1 dot = _____ dots

•••• •••• – • =

4.

13 dots take away 3 dots = _____ dots

••••••• ••••••• – :• • =

5.

11 dots take away 7 dots = _____ dots

•••••• ••••• – ••••• ••• =

6.

12 dots take away 12 dots = _____ dots

•••••• •••••• – •••••• •••••• =

Falling Leaves

Count the number of leaves in each group. Subtract the second group from the first. Write the number sentence.

1.

Group 1	Group 2

_____ – _____ = _____

2.

Group 1	Group 2

_____ – _____ = _____

3.

Group 1	Group 2

_____ – _____ = _____

4.

Group 1	Group 2

_____ – _____ = _____

5.

Group 1	Group 2

_____ – _____ = _____

6.

Group 1	Group 2

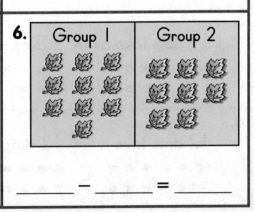

_____ – _____ = _____

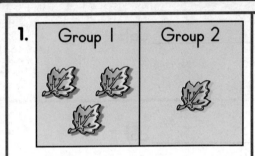

How Many Are Left?

Write a number sentence to go with each picture. Your answer will show how many are not crossed out.

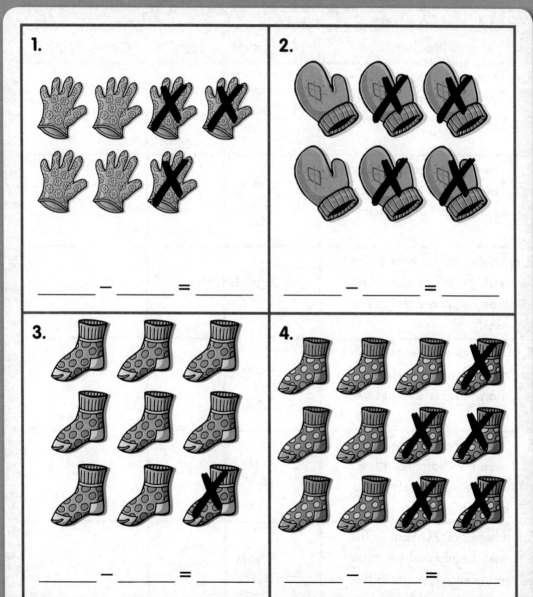

1.

____ − ____ = ____

2.

____ − ____ = ____

3.

____ − ____ = ____

4.

____ − ____ = ____

Left in the Nest

Solve each problem. Complete the chart. In the "Left?" column, tell how many eggs still need to hatch. Then draw that many.

	Problem	Hatched	Left?	Draw Them
1.	There are 6 eggs in the nest. Three hatched. How many eggs are left in the nest?	3		
2.	There are 8 eggs in the nest. Two hatched. How many eggs are left in the nest?	2		
3.	There are 10 eggs in the nest. Four hatched. How many eggs are left in the nest?	4		
4.	There are 12 eggs in the nest. One hatched. How many eggs are left in the nest?	—		
5.	There are 15 eggs in the nest. Five hatched. How many eggs are left in the nest?	—		
6.	There are 20 eggs in the nest. Eight hatched. How many eggs are left in the nest?	—		

Lucky Fours

How many leaves are there on a four-leaf clover? There are four, of course! Each time you see a four-leaf clover in one of the problems below, add or subtract 4. Solve each problem.

1.
$$\begin{array}{r} 1 \\ + \quad \text{} \\ \hline \end{array}$$

2.
$$\begin{array}{r} \text{} \\ + \quad 3 \\ \hline \end{array}$$

3.
$$\begin{array}{r} 6 \\ - \quad \text{} \\ \hline \end{array}$$

4.
$$\begin{array}{r} 8 \\ - \quad \text{} \\ \hline \end{array}$$

5.
$$\begin{array}{r} 7 \\ + \quad \text{} \\ \hline \end{array}$$

6.
$$\begin{array}{r} 7 \\ - \quad \text{} \\ \hline \end{array}$$

7.
$$\begin{array}{r} \text{} \\ + \quad 10 \\ \hline \end{array}$$

8.
$$\begin{array}{r} 13 \\ - \quad \text{} \\ \hline \end{array}$$

9.

= _____

10. + +

= _____

23

What Colors Do You See?

The balloons below need to be colored. Solve the problems. Follow the instructions to color each balloon.

The blue balloons have the answer to

$$9 - 0 =$$

The red balloons have the answer to

$$10 - 5 =$$

The green balloons have the answer to

$$12 - 6 =$$

The purple balloons have the answer to

$$11 - 4 =$$

What's In the Box?

Each box contains a number. Do the math to figure out each number. Then use those numbers to solve addition and subtraction problems.

 = 6 + 9, which equals [ ]   = 12 – 6, which equals [ ]

 = 7 + 3, which equals [ ]

1.

+

Write the number sentence.

_____ + _____ = _____

2.

–

Write the number sentence.

_____ – _____ = _____

3.

+

Write the number sentence.

_____ + _____ = _____

4.

–

Write the number sentence.

_____ – _____ = _____

5.

–

Write the number sentence.

_____ – _____ = _____

Add and Match

Add up the problems on the left. Draw lines to match the problems to the answers on the right.

7 + 4 =	9
9 + 5 =	11
5 + 11 =	12
10 + 10 =	14
7 + 8 =	15
2 + 7 =	16
6 + 6 =	18
13 + 5 =	20

Subtract and Match

Subtract the problems on the left. Draw lines to match the problems to the answers on the right.

17 – 2 =

19 – 5 =

18 – 11 =

20 – 17 =

16 – 4 =

12 – 7 =

16 – 6 =

13 – 5 =

3

5

7

8

10

12

14

15

All On the Line

Use the number line to help you solve the word problems.

```
0  1  2  3  4  5  6  7  8  9  10  11  12  13  14  15  16  17  18  19  20
```

1. Start on 4. ⌒ Count forward 5.

What number are you on? I am on _____.

2. Start on 3. ⌒ Count forward 6.

What number are you on? I am on _____.

3. Start on 9. ⌒ Count forward 7.

What number are you on? I am on _____.

4. Start on 7. ⌒ Count forward 8.

What number are you on? I am on _____.

5. Start on 11. ⌒ Count forward 9.

What number are you on? I am on _____.

6. Start on 13. ⌒ Count forward 7.

What number are you on? I am on _____.

Hop Ahead to Add

Count forward to add. Put your finger where the frog is. Hop forward as many times as it says in the second number of the addition problem. Write the number you land on.

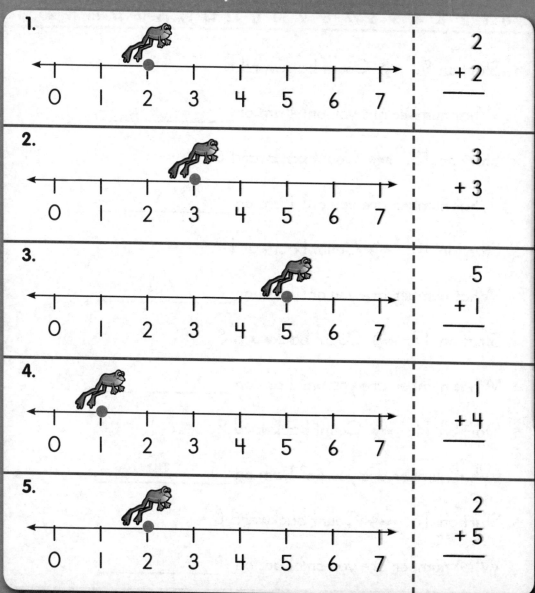

1.
0   1   2   3   4   5   6   7

2
+ 2
___

2.
0   1   2   3   4   5   6   7

3
+ 3
___

3.
0   1   2   3   4   5   6   7

5
+ 1
___

4.
0   1   2   3   4   5   6   7

1
+ 4
___

5.
0   1   2   3   4   5   6   7

2
+ 5
___

29

To the Back of the Line

Use the number line to help you solve the word problems.

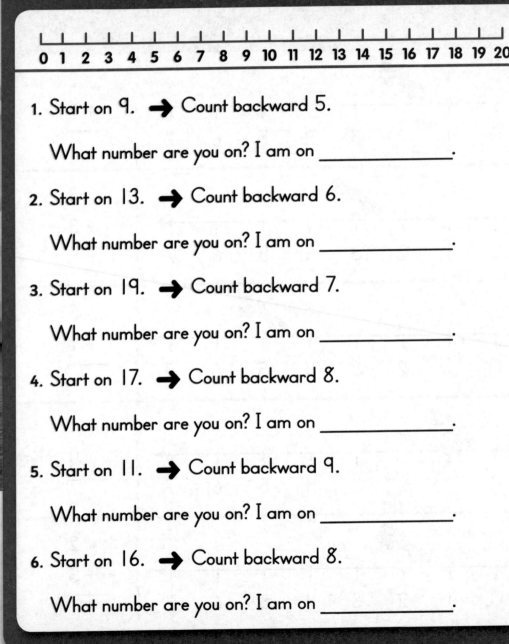

```
0  1  2  3  4  5  6  7  8  9  10  11  12  13  14  15  16  17  18  19  20
```

1. Start on 9. ➡ Count backward 5.

   What number are you on? I am on _____.

2. Start on 13. ➡ Count backward 6.

   What number are you on? I am on _____.

3. Start on 19. ➡ Count backward 7.

   What number are you on? I am on _____.

4. Start on 17. ➡ Count backward 8.

   What number are you on? I am on _____.

5. Start on 11. ➡ Count backward 9.

   What number are you on? I am on _____.

6. Start on 16. ➡ Count backward 8.

   What number are you on? I am on _____.

Jump Back to Subtract

Count backward to subtract. Put your finger where the kangaroo is. Jump backward as many times as it says in the second number of the subtraction problem. Write the number you land on.

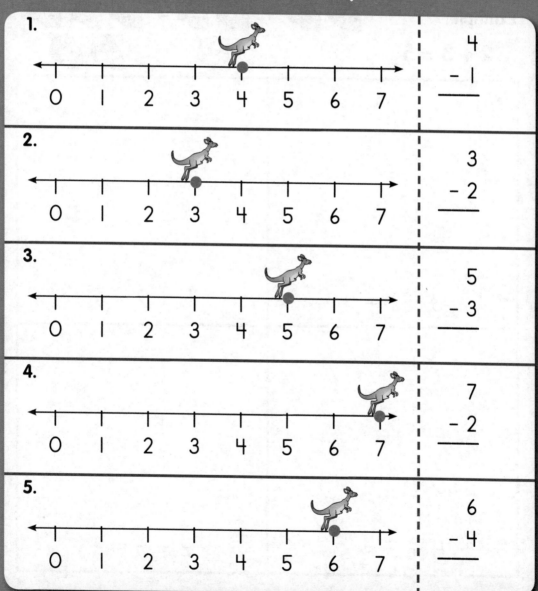

1.

0 1 2 3 4 5 6 7

$$\begin{array}{r} 4 \\ -\ 1 \\ \hline \end{array}$$

2.

0 1 2 3 4 5 6 7

$$\begin{array}{r} 3 \\ -\ 2 \\ \hline \end{array}$$

3.

0 1 2 3 4 5 6 7

$$\begin{array}{r} 5 \\ -\ 3 \\ \hline \end{array}$$

4.

0 1 2 3 4 5 6 7

$$\begin{array}{r} 7 \\ -\ 2 \\ \hline \end{array}$$

5.

0 1 2 3 4 5 6 7

$$\begin{array}{r} 6 \\ -\ 4 \\ \hline \end{array}$$

31

Drawing Addition

Draw a picture to show each number sentence. Use the example to help you.

Example:

$$2 + 3 = 5$$

🌰🌰 + 🌰🌰 = 🌰🌰🌰
🌰   🌰🌰

$3 + 1 = 4$	$5 + 2 = 7$
$4 + 3 = 7$	$2 + 6 = 8$

Drawing Subtraction

Draw a picture to show each number sentence. Use the example to help you.

Example:

3 – 1 = 2

4 – 2 = 2	5 – 4 = 1
6 – 3 = 3	8 – 4 = 4

Addition Wheels

Add the number in the center circle to each number in the middle circle. Write each sum in the outer circle. One is done for you.

1.

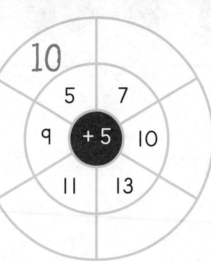

10

5   7

9   +5   10

11   13

2.

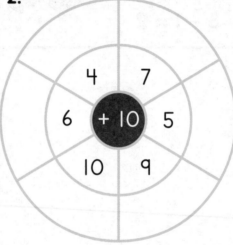

4   7

6   +10   5

10   9

3.

12   7

6   +7   5

11   9

4.

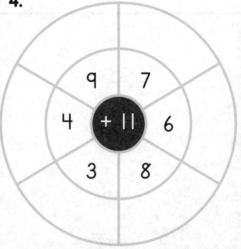

9   7

4   +11   6

3   8

Subtraction Wheels

Write the number in the middle circle so that when it is subtracted from the number in the outer circle, the difference is the number in the center. One is done for you.

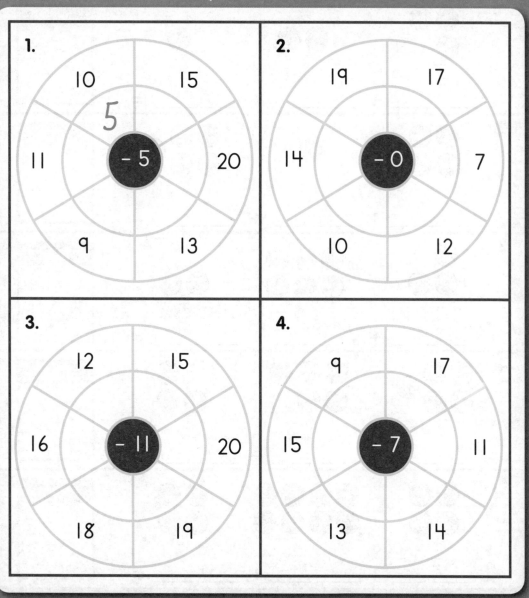

1.
10   15
5
11   − 5   20
9   13

2.
19   17
14   − 0   7
10   12

3.
12   15
16   − 11   20
18   19

4.
9   17
15   − 7   11
13   14

Have a Ball

Count each set of balls. Write the number. Add all the numbers together in each row. Write the total.

1.

Total

_____ + _____ + _____ =

2.

Total

_____ + _____ + _____ =

3.

Total

_____ + _____ + _____ =

4.

Total

_____ + _____ + _____ =

5.

Total

_____ + _____ + _____ =

Caps for Sale

There is a big sale on caps. Find out how much each cap will cost during the sale. Fill out the price chart.

Big Sale!

Take $2 off all red caps!   Take $4 off all green caps!
Take $3 off all blue caps!   Take $5 off all purple caps!

Price Chart			
Cap	Old Price	$$ Off	New Price
	$12		
	$15		
	$14		
	$14		

1. Which cap cost the least **before** the sale? Circle that cap.

2. Which cap costs the least **during** the sale? Circle that cap.

Adding and Subtracting

Does the problem have an addition sign (+) or a subtraction sign (–)? Use that clue to solve each problem.

1. $\begin{array}{r} 13 \\ -\ 3 \\ \hline \end{array}$	**2.** $\begin{array}{r} 13 \\ +\ 3 \\ \hline \end{array}$	**3.** $\begin{array}{r} 9 \\ -\ 4 \\ \hline \end{array}$	**4.** $\begin{array}{r} 8 \\ +\ 5 \\ \hline \end{array}$
5. $\begin{array}{r} 11 \\ +\ 9 \\ \hline \end{array}$	**6.** $\begin{array}{r} 16 \\ -\ 5 \\ \hline \end{array}$	**7.** $\begin{array}{r} 6 \\ +\ 8 \\ \hline \end{array}$	**8.** $\begin{array}{r} 17 \\ -\ 9 \\ \hline \end{array}$

Read each word problem below. What do you need to do to solve the problem? Circle add or subtract.

9. Ella had 12 glass beakers in her science kit. One of those beakers broke, and her friend borrowed another one. How many beakers does she have in her kit now?

add

subtract

10. Drew collects baseball cards. He had 10 cards of his favorite player. His cousin gave him 6 more of that player's cards. How many does he have now?

add

subtract

Fishing for Facts

Do the math. Check the correct box beneath each number sentence. If the number sentence doesn't add up, draw in fish to make it correct.

1.

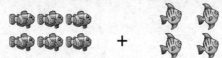 + = 10 fish

❑ It's correct!   ❑ It's wrong! I need to add fish.

2.

 + = 12 fish

❑ It's correct!   ❑ It's wrong! I need to add fish.

3.

 + 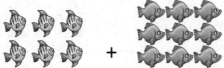 = 18 fish

❑ It's correct!   ❑ It's wrong! I need to add fish.

4.

 + = 17 fish

❑ It's correct!   ❑ It's wrong! I need to add fish.

5.

 + = 15 fish

❑ It's correct!   ❑ It's wrong! I need to add fish.

Count the Corners

Look at these shapes. How many corners or points does each shape have?

▲ = _____ corners   ☆ = _____ points   ■ = _____ corners

In the problems below, the shapes stand for the number of corners / points each one has. Use those numbers to solve the addition and subtraction problems.

1.

▲ + ■ =

_____ + _____ = _____

2.

☆ + ■ =

_____ + _____ = _____

3.

☆ - ■ =

_____ - _____ = _____

4.

☆ + ▲ =

_____ + _____ = _____

5.

▲ + ☆ + ■ =

_____ + _____ + _____ = _____

6.

▲ + ▲ + ☆ - ■ - ■ =

_____ + _____ + _____ - _____ - _____ = _____

Plus and Minus Puzzle

Solve the addition and subtraction problems. Write the number names from the Number Bank in the puzzle below.

Across
1. 13 – 7 =
2. 5 + 6 =
4. 9 + 4 =
5. 20 – 20 =

Down
1. 12 + 5 =
2. 18 – 10 =
3. 4 + 4 + 1 =
6. 11 – 10 =

Number Bank

zero

one

six

eight

nine

eleven

thirteen

seventeen

Money Addition

Use addition to find out how much money is in each row.

Remember:

 = 1¢   = 5¢   = 10¢   = 25¢

1. + (pennies) =

2. + + =

3. + =

4. + + =

5. + + =

6. + + =

Money Subtraction

Use subtraction to find out how much more one group of coins is then another.

Remember:

 = 1¢ = 5¢ = 10¢ = 25¢

1.

 −   =

2.

  −   −   =

3.

 − =

4.

 −   =

5.

  −   −   =

6.

   −   −   =

Get the Scoop

On a hot, summer day, two local schools sold ice cream.
Solve each problem to get the correct amount of scoops sold.

1. Elm School sold 20 scoops of vanilla, 10 scoops of chocolate, and 7 scoops of mint chip. Write the number sentence to show how many scoops they sold all together.

_____ + _____ + _____ = _____

2. Pine School sold 15 scoops of vanilla, 20 scoops of chocolate, and 5 scoops of mint chip. Write the number sentence to show how many scoops they sold all together.

_____ + _____ + _____ = _____

3. Circle the school that sold more scoops of vanilla.

   Write a number sentence to show how many more they sold.

   Elm

   Pine

4. Circle the school that sold more scoops of mint chip?

   Write a number sentence to show how many more they sold.

   Elm

   Pine

5. Circle the school that sold more total scoops?

   Write a number sentence to show how many more they sold.

   Elm

   Pine

Cookie Math

Sara is selling five different small cookies at her bake sale. Use these prices to solve the problems below.

12¢   6¢   10¢   8¢   15¢

1. Jay bought 2 [triangle] [triangle] and 1 [moon] . How much did he spend?

_____ + _____ + _____ = _____

2. Becca bought 2 [star] [star] , 1 [moon] , and 1 [triangle] . How much did she spend?

_____ + _____ + _____ + _____ = _____

3. Marla bought 2 [star] [star] , 1 [star] , 1 [rectangle] , and 1 [triangle] . How much did she spend?

_____ + _____ + _____ + _____ + _____ =

4. Which of these friends spent more?

Nick bought 4 [star] [star] [star] [star] . Lulu bought 1 [rectangle] and 2 [triangle] [triangle] .

Show your work

Give Your Answer

Nick spent _____.

Lulu spent _____.

_____ spent more.

45

Equal Sides

The equations on both sides of the equal sign need to equal each other. Write in the missing addend that will make them equal. When you use an addend, shade it in here:

0 1 2 3 4 5 6 7 8 9

1. $3 + 4 = \boxed{} + 3$

2. $5 + 4 = 4 + \boxed{}$

3. $2 + 9 = \boxed{} + 2$

4. $3 + 3 = 0 + \boxed{}$

5. $7 + 2 = \boxed{} + 1$

6. $5 + 5 = 9 + \boxed{}$

7. $4 + 4 = 1 + \boxed{}$

8. $7 - 4 = 6 - \boxed{}$

9. $10 - 5 = 5 + \boxed{}$

10. $2 + 2 = 6 - \boxed{}$

Write Your Own: Try writing one of your own. Write addition or subtraction problems that equal each other. Put them on opposite sides of the equal sign.

_____ _____ = _____ _____

Back and Forth

Use the number line to help you solve the word problems.

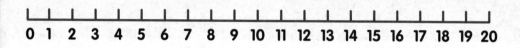

1. Start on 8. ➡ Count forward 4. Count backward 5.

   What number are you on? I am on _____.

2. Start on 13. ➡ Count forward 6. Count backward 2.

   What number are you on? I am on _____.

3. Start on 19. ➡ Count backward 7. Count forward 1.

   What number are you on? I am on _____.

4. Start on 17. ➡ Count backward 8. Count forward 9.

   What number are you on? I am on _____.

5. Start on 11. ➡ Count backward 9. Count forward 12.

   What number are you on? I am on _____.

6. Start on 6. ➡ Count forward 14. Count backward 10.

   What number are you on? I am on _____.

An Odd and Even Quilt

Solve each addition or subtraction problem.
- If the answer is odd, color the space yellow.
- If the answer is even, color the space green.

$7 + 7 =$	$5 - 2 =$	$4 - 4 =$	$13 + 2 =$
$14 - 2 =$	$9 + 5 =$	$16 - 1 =$	$5 + 11 =$
$1 + 5 =$	$13 - 6 =$	$6 + 4 =$	$0 + 19 =$
$13 - 0 =$	$17 + 3 =$	$9 + 2 =$	$12 - 6 =$
$21 - 1 =$	$11 - 10 =$	$13 - 5 =$	$14 + 3 =$
$14 - 3 =$	$3 + 9 =$	$2 + 15 =$	$18 - 13 =$
$10 + 10 =$	$6 - 3 =$	$10 - 10 =$	$19 + 1 =$
$17 - 2 =$	$7 - 7 =$	$11 + 6 =$	$19 - 1 =$

If/Then Quilt

Solve each addition or subtraction problem.
- If the answer is < 10, color the space red.
- If the answer is > 20, color the space purple.
- If the answer is from 10–20, color the space yellow.

11 − 10	8 + 8	20 + 2	13 − 3	15 + 10	20 − 16
3 + 21	20 − 19	9 + 9	7 + 1	13 + 3	1 + 24
12 − 0	25 − 2	30 − 30	14 + 4	10 + 20	18 − 8
9 + 11	8 + 0	7 + 4	7 + 14	10 − 1	19 − 1
6 + 6	6 + 16	15 − 10	18 − 0	21 − 20	28 − 2
20 − 0	22 − 10	1 + 7	0 + 0	0 + 13	17 + 8

Show of Hands

Each hand has 5 fingers. Write number sentences and show how you can add by multiples of 5.

1.

_____ fingers + _____ fingers = _____ fingers

2.

_____ fingers + _____ fingers = _____ fingers

3.

_____ fingers + _____ fingers = _____ fingers

4.

_____ fingers + _____ fingers = _____ fingers

5.

_____ fingers + _____ fingers = _____ fingers

6.

_____ fingers + _____ fingers = _____ fingers

A Dozen Donuts

Donuts are often sold by the dozen. There are 12 in a dozen. Look at each set of donuts. Write in how many more are needed to make a dozen.

1.

 + _____ = 12

2.

+ _____ = 12

3.

 _____ + = 12

4.

_____ + = 12

5.

 + _____ = 12

6. Look at the group of donuts below. Draw more donuts so that there are a dozen in the group.

Hat Trick

Look under each hat. Which one has the correct math fact? Circle that hat. Cross out the wrong number sentence and rewrite it with the correct answer.

1.

13 + 5 = 19 | 12 − 3 = 9

New number sentence:

_____

2.

14 + 6 = 20 | 14 − 6 = 6

New number sentence:

_____

3.

9 + 8 = 18 | 20 − 7 = 13

New number sentence:

_____

4.

18 + 4 = 24 | 14 − 4 = 10

New number sentence:

_____

5.

16 + 5 = 21 | 13 − 11 = 3

New number sentence:

_____

6.

15 + 7 = 22 | 22 − 15 = 9

New number sentence:

_____

Party Problems

Patty and Paulo are planning a party for Penny. Use addition or subtraction to solve these word problems. Write the number sentence and answer for each.

1. Patty found 15 party hats. There will be 25 people at the party, and each one needs a hat. How many more hats does Penny need?

_____ _____ _____

Answer: _____ more hats

2. Penny's favorite colors are red and gold. Paulo blew up 12 gold balloons. Patty blew up 6 red ones. How many did the two blow up all together?

_____ _____ _____

Answer: _____ balloons

3. Patty can spend $11 more on the party. Paulo can spend $8. How much money do the two friends have for the party?

_____ _____ _____

Answer: _____ for the party

4. Patty and Paulo want to spend about $15 on a cake. They found the perfect one for $13. How much less does that cake cost than what they planned to spend?

_____ _____ _____

Answer: _____ less

What's Missing?

Look at the problems below. What's missing? Does the number sentence need a plus sign (+) or a minus sign (−)? Write in the missing sign.

1.
16 ☐ 4 = 20

2.
16 ☐ 4 = 12

3.
22 ☐ 7 = 15

4.
13 ☐ 6 = 7

5.
25 ☐ 10 = 15

6.
25 ☐ 10 = 35

7.
8 ☐ 4 ☐ 3 = 15

8.
8 ☐ 4 ☐ 3 = 1

Challenge!
8 ☐ 4 ☐ 3 = 7

Can you write a "What's Missing?" problem of your own? Write a number sentence of your own. Leave out the plus or minus sign. See if someone you know can solve it!

_____ ☐ _____ = _____

Color Wheel

Use the numbers on this color wheel to write number sentences and solve problems.

9
7
13
12
6
10

1. red + blue = ?

_____ + _____ = _____

2. purple + yellow = ?

_____ + _____ = _____

3. green + orange = ?

_____ + _____ = _____

4. red − blue = ?

_____ − _____ = _____

5. orange − yellow = ?

_____ − _____ = _____

6. green − purple = ?

_____ − _____ = _____

7. green + blue + orange = ?

_____ + _____ + _____ = _____

Two in One

Each of these word problems can be used to solve an addition and a subtraction problem. See if you can solve them all!

 Alan ate 12 bowls of cereal this month. He also ate 7 pieces of toast, 11 waffles, and 4 bowls of oatmeal.

1. How many bowls of food (cereal and oatmeal) did he eat all together? _____

2. How many more waffles did he eat than pieces of toast? _____

 Ceci sold 11 bags of chips during lunchtime on Monday. She sold 5 more on Tuesday, 8 on Wednesday, and 14 on Thursday.

3. How many more bags of chips did she sell on Thursday than on Tuesday? _____

4. How many bags of chips did she sell all together on Monday, Tuesday, and Wednesday? _____

 Marco makes the best hot cocoa in town. He made 20 cups of cocoa for his friends in November. He made 23 cups for his friends in December. In January he made as many cups as he had made in November and December combined!

5. How many cups of cocoa did Marco make in January? _____

6. How many fewer cups did he make in December than in January? _____

Math for the Ages

Lily is the youngest child of four children in her family, and she is turning one today. Use your addition and subtraction skills to determine the ages of the other members of her family.

1. Lily's brother Ben is four years older than his baby sister. How old is Ben? _____

2. Annie is the oldest child in Lily's family. She's 12 years older than the family's youngest child. How old is Annie? _____

3. Nicky is four years older than his brother Ben, but four years younger than his oldest sister. How old is Nicky? _____

4. Lily's mother is 25 years older than her oldest child. How old is Lily's mother? _____

5. Lily's father is two years younger than Lily's mother. How old is Lily's father? _____

6. If you add up the ages of the four children in Lily's family, what total do you get?

Show Your Work	Answer

Score By Sevens

Can you make your way through the maze to score a touchdown? Only draw a line through problems with an answer of 7. Follow the 7s and score!

Figure Eights

Solve the problems in the picture.
- If the answer is 8, color the space orange.
- If the answer is more than 8, color the space blue.
- If the answer is less than 8, color the space brown.

Look at the addition boxes below. Add up any set of numbers in any row or column. The answer is always 11. But some of the numbers are missing! Can you figure out which numbers need to be written in and where? Remember, all sets of numbers going across or down must add up to 11.

1.

3	4		= 11
	5	2	= 11
4		5	= 11
= 11	= 11	= 11	

2.

6		1	= 11
	3		= 11
5		2	= 11
= 11	= 11	= 11	

3.

	5	4	= 11
			= 11
3	6		= 11
= 11	= 11	= 11	

4.

9		0	= 11
	7		= 11
		8	= 11
= 11	= 11	= 11	

5.

7	1		= 11
		3	= 11
	4		= 11
= 11	= 11	= 11	

6.

3			= 11
	6		= 11
	3	0	= 11
= 11	= 11	= 11	

Word's Worth

Look at the Points Box. Each letter of the alphabet has been given a point value. To find the total value of a word, add up the point values of all of the letters in that word. Write the number sentence to show how you found the total.

Here's an example for the word be:

b	e	Total
2	5	2 + 5 = 7

Points Box

a = 1
b = 2
c = 3
d = 4
e = 5
f = 6
g = 7
h = 8
i = 9
j = 10
k = 11
l = 12
m = 13
n = 14
o = 15
p = 16
q = 17
r = 18
s = 19
t = 20
u = 21
v = 22
w = 23
x = 24
y = 25
z = 26

Word	Number Sentence
an	_____ + _____ = _____
do	_____ + _____ = _____
we	_____ + _____ = _____
my	_____ + _____ = _____
cab	_____ + _____ + _____ = _____
day	_____ + _____ + _____ = _____
hen	_____ + _____ + _____ = _____
fox	_____ + _____ + _____ = _____
jet	_____ + _____ + _____ = _____

61

Answer Key

"Button Up" (page 8)
1. 4, 2. 3, 3. 5, 4. 4, 5. 5, 6. 6

"Adding Hearts" (page 9)
1. 3, 2. 5, 3. 4, 4. 6, 5. 7, 6. 6

"Adding Apples" (page 10)
1. 6, 2. 9, 3. 10, 4. 14, 5. 13, 6. 16

"Let It Snow" (page 11)
1. 8, 2. 10, 3. 11, 4. 12, 5. 18
Draw your own: 2 + 5 = 7

"Time for Bed" (page 12)
8 + 3 = 11, 0 + 10 = 10, 7 + 5 = 12, 9 + 4 = 13

"A Sum of 20" (page 13)
10—10, 12—8, 7—13, 14—6, 20—0, 3—17, 15—5, 9—11

"Math Machines" (page 14)
1. 9, 8, 10, 12, 14; 2. 4, 6, 8, 16, 13; 3. 19, 11, 18, 20, 15; 4. 3, 5, 15, 11, 9, 6; 5. 18, 19, 21, 22, 20, 24; 6. 10, 1, 11, 2, 9, 4

"Odd or Even?" (page 15)
1. odd, red; 2. even, green; 3. even, green; 4. even, green; 5. odd, red; 6. odd, red; 7. even, green; 8. odd, red; 9. odd, red; 10. even, green; 11. odd, red; 12. odd, red

"More or Less?" (page 16)
1. <, 2. >, 3. <, 4. =, 5. >, 6. <, 7. =, 8. <, 9. >, 10. <, 11. >, 12. =

"Mixed-Up More or Less?" (page 17)
1. <, 2. <, 3. >, 4. =, 5. >, 6. >, 7. <, 8. =, 9. <, 10. >, 11. <, 12. =

"Adding Dots" (page 18)
1. 6, 2. 8, 3. 9, 4. 12, 5. 15, 6. 20

"Subtracting Dots" (page 19)
1. 2, 2. 1, 3. 7, 4. 10, 5. 4, 6. 0

"Falling Leaves" (page 20)
1. 3 – 1 = 2, 2. 6 – 2 = 4, 3. 4 – 4 = 0, 4. 8 – 3 = 5, 5. 7 – 6 = 1, 6. 10 – 8 = 2

"How Many Are Left?" (page 21)
1. 7 – 3 = 4, 2. 6 – 4 = 2, 3. 9 – 1 = 8, 4. 12 – 5 = 7

"Left in the Nest" (page 22)
1. 3; 2. 6; 3. 6; 4. 1, 11; 5. 5, 10; 6. 8, 12

"Lucky Fours" (page 23)
1. 5, 2. 7, 3. 2, 4. 4, 5. 11, 6. 3, 7. 14, 8. 9, 9. 0, 10. 12

"What Colors Do You See?" (page 24)
Students should color 9s blue, 5s red, 6s green, and 7s purple.

"What's In the Box?" (page 25)
yellow: 15, blue: 6, pink: 10; 1. 15 + 6 = 21, 2. 10 – 6 = 4, 3. 6 + 10 = 16, 4. 15 – 10 = 5, 5. 15 – 6 = 9

"Add and Match" (page 26)
7 + 4 = 11, 9 + 5 = 14, 5 + 11 = 16, 10 + 10 = 20, 7 + 8 = 15, 2 + 7 = 9, 6 + 6 = 12, 13 + 5 = 18

"Subtract and Match" (page 27)
17 – 2 = 15, 19 – 5 = 14, 18 – 11 = 7, 20 – 17 = 3, 16 – 4 = 12, 12 – 7 = 5, 16 – 6 = 10, 13 – 5 = 8

"All On the Line" (page 28)
1. 9, 2. 9, 3. 16, 4. 15, 5. 20, 6. 20

"Hop Ahead to Add" (page 29)
1. 4, 2. 6, 3. 6, 4. 5, 5. 7

"To the Back of the Line" (page 30)
1. 4, 2. 7, 3. 12, 4. 9, 5. 2, 6. 8

"Jump Back to Subtract" (page 31)
1. 3, 2. 1, 3. 2, 4. 5, 5. 2

"Addition Wheels" (page 34)
clockwise from top right: 1. 12, 15, 18, 16, 14, 10; 2. 17, 15, 19, 20, 16, 14; 3. 14, 12, 16, 18, 13, 19; 4. 18, 17, 19, 14, 15, 20

"Subtraction Wheels" (page 35)
clockwise from top right: 1. 10, 15, 8, 4, 6, 5; 2. 17, 7, 12, 10, 14, 19; 3. 4, 9, 8, 7, 5, 1; 4. 10, 4, 7, 6, 8, 2

"Have a Ball" (page 36)
1. 3 + 2 + 1 = 6, 2. 4 + 1 + 5 = 10, 3. 3 + 6 + 2 = 11, 4. 5 + 5 + 3 = 13, 5. 4 + 8 + 4 = 16

"Caps for Sale" (page 37)

Cap	Old Price	$$ Off	New Price
red	$12	$2	$10
green	$15	$4	$11
blue	$14	$3	$11
purple	$14	$5	$9

1. red cap, 2. purple cap

"Adding and Subtracting" (page 38)
1. 10
2. 16
3. 5
4. 13
5. 20
6. 11
7. 14
8. 8
9. subtract
10. add

"Fishing for Facts" (page 39)
1. correct
2. wrong, draw in 2 fish
3. wrong, draw in 3 fish
4. correct
5. wrong, draw in 3 fish

"Count the Corners" (page 40)
1. 3 + 4 = 7, 2. 5 + 4 = 9, 3. 5 − 4 = 1, 4. 5 + 3 = 8, 5.
3 + 5 + 4 = 12, 6. 3 + 3 + 5 − 4 − 4 = 3

"Plus and Minus Puzzle" (page 41)

"Money Addition" (page 42)
1. 20¢ + 10¢ = 30¢, 2. 10¢ + 15¢ + 5¢ = 30¢,
3. 25¢ + 10¢ = 35¢, 4. 25¢ + 30¢ + 2¢ = 57¢,
5. 50¢ + 40¢ + 7¢ = 97¢, 6. 30¢ + 15¢ + 4¢ = 49¢

"Money Subtraction" (page 43)
1. 20¢ − 10¢ = 10¢, 2. 40¢ − 15¢ − 5¢ = 20¢,
3. 25¢ − 10¢ = 15¢, 4. 50¢ − 30¢ − 4¢ = 16¢,
5. 50¢ − 40¢ − 8¢ = 2¢, 6. 30¢ − 15¢ − 6¢ = 9¢

"Get the Scoop" (page 44)
1. 20 + 10 + 7 = 37, 2. 15 + 20 + 5 = 40, 3. Elm,
20 − 15 = 5, 4. Elm, 7 − 5 = 2, 5. Pine, 40 − 37 = 3

"Cookie Math" (page 45)
1. 10¢ + 10¢ + 6¢ = 26¢; 2. 8¢ + 8¢ + 6¢ + 10¢ = 32¢;
3. 12¢ + 12¢ + 8¢ + 15¢ + 10¢ = 57¢; 4. Nick: 8¢ + 8¢
+ 8¢ + 8¢ = 32¢, Lulu: 15¢ + 10¢ + 10¢ = 35¢, Lulu
spent more.

"Equal Sides" (page 46)
1. 4, 2. 5, 3. 9, 4. 6, 5. 8, 6. 1, 7. 7, 8. 3, 9. 0, 10. 2

"Back and Forth" (page 47)
1. 7, 2. 17, 3. 13, 4. 18, 5. 14, 6. 10

"Show of Hands" (page 50)
1. 5 + 10 = 15, 2. 10 + 15 = 25, 3. 20 + 10 = 30,
4. 5 + 20 = 25, 5. 15 + 15 = 30, 6. 25 + 10 = 35

"A Dozen Donuts" (page 51)
1. 2, 2. 9, 3. 6, 4. 11, 5. 8, 6. Draw five donuts.

"Hat Trick" (page 52)
1. correct: 12 − 3 = 9, new: 13 + 5 = 18; 2. correct: 14
+ 6 = 20, new: 14 − 6 = 8; 3. correct: 20 − 7 = 13,
new: 9 + 8 = 17; 4. correct: 14 − 4 = 10, new: 18 +
4 = 22; 5. correct: 16 + 5 = 21, new: 13 − 11 = 2;
6. correct: 15 + 7 = 22, new: 22 − 15 = 7

"Party Problems" (page 53)
1. 25 − 15 = 10 more hats; 2. 12 + 6 = 18 balloons;
3. 11 + 8 = $19; 4. 15 − 13 = $2 less

"What's Missing?" (page 54)
1. +; 2. −; 3. −; 4. −; 5. −; 6. +; 7. +, +; 8. −, −;
Challenge: −, +

"Color Wheel" (page 55)
1. 12 + 9 = 21, 2. 7 + 6 = 13, 3. 13 + 10 = 23,
4. 12 − 9 = 3, 5. 10 − 6 = 4, 6. 13 − 7 = 6,
7. 13 + 9 + 10 = 32

"Two in One" (page 56)
1. 12 + 4 = 16, 2. 11 − 7 = 4, 3. 14 − 5 = 9,
4. 11 + 5 + 8 = 24, 5. 20 + 23 = 43, 6. 43 − 23 = 20

"Math for the Ages" (page 57)
1. 5, 2. 13, 3. 9, 4. 38, 5. 36, 6. 1 (Lily) + 5 (Ben) + 9
(Nicky) + 13 (Annie) = 28

"These Go to 11" (page 60)

1.
3	4	**4**	11
4	5	2	11
4	**2**	5	11
11	11	11	

2.
6	**4**	1	11
0	3	8	11
5	**4**	2	11
11	11	11	

3.
2	5	4	11
6	0	5	11
3	6	**2**	11
11	11	11	

4.
9	**2**	0	11
1	**7**	3	11
1	2	8	11
11	11	11	

5.
7	1	**3**	11
2	6	3	11
2	**4**	5	11
11	11	11	

6.
3	**2**	6	11
0	6	5	11
8	3	0	11
11	11	11	

"Word's Worth" (page 61)
an: 1 + 14 = 15; do: 4 + 15 = 19; we: 23 + 5 = 28;
my: 13 + 25 = 38; cab: 3 + 1 + 2 = 6; day: 4 + 1 + 25
= 30; hen: 8 + 5 + 14 = 27; fox: 6 + 15 + 24 = 45;
jet: 10 + 5 + 20 = 35